THE BEGINNER'S HANDBOOK OF
DOWSING

THE BEGINNER'S HANDBOOK OF
DOWSING

THE ANCIENT ART OF DIVINING
UNDERGROUND WATER SOURCES

by Joseph Baum
with illustrations by the author

CROWN PUBLISHERS, INC., NEW YORK

Library of Congress Catalog Card Number: 73-89055

Printed in the United States of America
Published simultaneously in Canada by General Publishing Company Limited
Second Printing, October, 1974

dowse . . . [origin unknown] : to use the divining rod (as in search of water or ore) . . . to find (as water) by dowsing.

From *Webster's Third New International Dictionary*

Introduction

Dowsing (water witching or water divining) is probably as old as man's need for water. It is an "art" certain people have which enables them to find underground sources of water. The dowser can determine where the water is, as well as its depth and volume. There is no trickery or chicanery involved.

Why, it might be asked, doesn't everyone have this gift? Why only certain people? I honestly don't know. Wild animals in the bush can "smell" a waterhole miles away. A bloodhound has the ability to locate missing objects or people. Perhaps the ability to dowse is the vestige of some such animal instinct that only a few civilized men still possess. Perhaps this is why it is often referred to as radiesthesia—a sensitivity to the radiations that emanate from everything around us, including people, minerals, water, and so on. The whole phenomenon of dowsing interested Albert Einstein, who believed that some day electromagnetism might be found to hold the answers. Professor Joseph B. Rhine of Duke University has suggested that dowsing has more to do with ESP (extra-sensory perception) than physics. Whatever the truth, in the words of the French physiologist and Nobel Prize winner Charles Richet: "Dowsing is a fact we must accept."

And many people have accepted it, including government agencies and private corporations. In 1931 the government of British Columbia, Canada, employed a dowser (a woman!) to locate water for the widely scattered homesteads in that area. The Bristol-Myers Company paid $2,500 to a dowser for his efforts in locating a water supply for their new plant in New Jersey. The dowser located an underground stream capable of supplying 175 gallons of water a minute. Canadian Industries, partly owned by the E. I. du Pont de Nemours Company, also paid a dowser $2,500 for his help in finding an adequate source of water. And RCA paid a dowser handsomely for the same service for their Victor plant in New Jersey.

There are more potential dowsers than one might think. I have witnessed demonstrations where almost half the group, to their surprise, discovered that they were dowsers. More often, however, only about one in ten seems to feel the tug of the forked branch. The other nine, who experience no such phenomenon, are ready to call that one a fake! So either you have the gift or you don't.

How does one know if he has the gift of dowsing? You can find fascinating answers in the folklore surrounding the subject. "The power

The diviner at work. From an engraving, 1875. Note the unusual grip the dowser employs. Chapter 8 features other types of rods and how to hold them.

is inherited from mother to son or from father to daughter." "You must be the seventh son of a seventh son." "Only a chosen few are handed this gift of divination from above . . . or from the Devil below."

Here is how I discovered I was a dowser. About twenty-five years ago while living and farming in a small village high in the Berkshires, I made the acquaintance of a retired chemist who spent part of his summers there. He was in his eighties, a graduate of Rutgers in 1891, a member of the American Chemical Society and the holder of the first U.S. patent for processing lead arsenate for agricultural use. I was raising bees for honey at the time. This gentleman had also raised bees many years before, and the highlight of his visits was when he joined me working with them. We would have a great time going through the hives, following the queen from cell to cell as she deposited her eggs, checking the brood, and just watching all the fascinating things that bees do.

One evening at a little get-together my friend was holding forth on the great visionaries of the past. He mentioned Moses as possibly the first dowser in history. When he finished his discourse I asked him if he really believed in dowsing. He not only believed but also considered himself a darn good dowser! I must say that although the old gent was serious most of the time, a little impish humor would occasionally surface. This was one of those occasions, I thought. I knew nothing about dowsing and quite frankly I was very, very skeptical. He suggested that it might be both fun and educational to hold a dowsing party the next morning. We all agreed.

Ten of us showed up the next morning and we found our host ready and eager, with a dozen willow branches to use as rods. (His son later told me that his father was up at 5 a.m. cutting just the right branches.) We were all shown how to hold the rod, and at his direction we formed a single line with him at the head. We marched slowly around the yard, leader and skeptics, each holding his rod straight out as instructed. I was third in line and enjoyed every bit of this. Around the yard we marched and all I could think of was how completely ludicrous we must have looked to the passing motorists.

Suddenly our leader stopped and shouted, "There's a very strong pull here." I stepped out of line to see more clearly what had happened.

There he was with his rod pulled down to a vertical position. I remember thinking that his rod dipped because he loosened his grip and gravity took care of the rest. A little of that pixie humor. The line was ordered to continue, and while these thoughts were with me I arrived at the spot where our dowser had played his practical joke. At that moment, without warning, the tip of my rod bent down so violently as to twist the bark off the twig where I held it in my hands. I don't ever recall a feeling quite like the one I experienced that morning. There I was, viewing this whole operation so very lightly, when suddenly some strange force had reached up to pull the tip of the rod down with enough power to rupture the bark! That cool sensation at the base of my neck finally disappeared and I emerged from the experience with an entirely different attitude about dowsing.

Of the ten who participated only two were dowsers, my wife and I. She was particularly intrigued because her rod kept going up instead of down. (Some claim that when the rod goes up, it signifies still water or bad water, but others argue that dowsing is dowsing regardless of how the rod reacts. To this day the rod that my wife holds will go up at all the places where my rod goes down.)

Today there seems to be a great interest in dowsing. Perhaps it is because more and more people are beginning to appreciate the value and rarity of the pure, sparkling water that one finds in underground springs and streams. This handbook is for the person who is curious about the ancient art of dowsing, the person who wants a beginner's guide to show and explain in detail the technique of dowsing.

Are you a dowser? You will never know until you try.

". . . and Moses . . . smote the rock with his rod and water came forth abundantly."
Numbers 20:11

2 The rod

The rod used for dowsing can be as simple as a forked branch or as complex as electronic gear. Wire clothes hangers, copper and nylon rods, are also used. The pendulum, that ancient magic device, is a popular dowsing device in Europe. It consists of a weight on a string, and this weight can be of such materials as wood, metal, or objects like keys, etc. At one time a German sausage joined the list of dowsing materials. There have also been dowsers who used just their hands and no rods. They merely held out both their hands in front of them with open palms down and walked until a pull on the hands was felt.

For the beginner, however, a freshly cut forked branch should do

The many rod
possibilities
in a typical
limb formation.

nicely. All small twigs should be removed. It should be pliable so that it bends rather than breaks when the end is pulled down. A rod of willow, young maple, or a branch of any common tree will do as long as it is pliable. I recommend that the rod have the diameter of a pencil and be about eighteen inches long. Rods have been known to vary in diameter from one-eighth to one-half inch and to be as long as thirty inches.

Some old-timers will swear that witch-hazel rods are best. Other dowsers claim that nothing works as well as copper rods. As you become more practiced in the art you will of course select a rod that for you will be the most comfortable to work with.

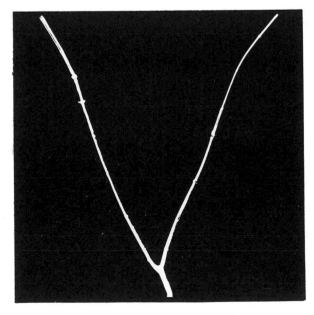

The rod, cleared of twigs and leaves, ready for dowsing.

3 | The grip

Grasp the branch by the tapering forks, palms up. Rest your clenched fists on your hips. The tip of the branch should point straight out, slightly higher than level. The forks should be held firmly enough to prevent the tip from bending down as a result of gravity. After a little practice you will be able to judge how tight the grip should be.

There are other ways of gripping the dowsing rod. If you find that you are a dowser, you would, I am sure, want to experiment with various grips until you found the one most suited to your particular style. Described and illustrated here is the grip that works best for me.

Rest the rod against the open hands.

Close the hands around the rod.

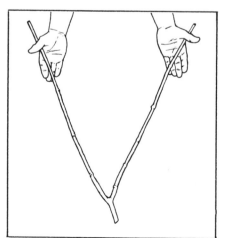
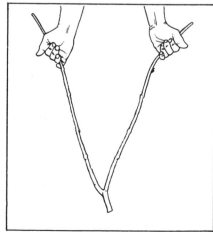

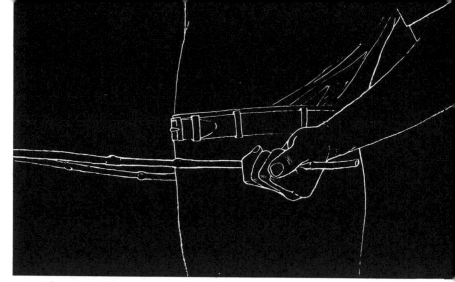

Fists tight to sides. For some, it might work better to have the elbows close to the sides with the fists slightly forward.

Holding the rod as shown, swing it upward until the end is slightly higher than the forks at your side.

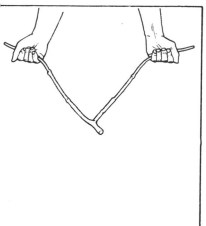

The practice of dowsing

A series of pictures showing the author dowsing.   Notice how the rod gradually bends

Holding the rod properly, walk with even, deliberate steps over the area to be dowsed. Do not lift your legs too high while walking. Keep your feet close to the ground, just avoiding a shuffle.

If you are a dowser and you pass over an underground water supply, the end of the rod will suddenly be pulled downward to a vertical position. The pull can be so strong as to rupture the bark or even break the rod at the point where you are holding it. If your eyes were closed you might even imagine that someone had actually taken the end and

14

om a horizontal to a vertical position as you near the source of water.   With some dowsers the rod goes up instead of down.

forced it down.

When the rod has signaled the spot, put in a stake or marker at the Point of Greatest Pull. If you approach the spot from different directions you might find that this point varies slightly. If this happens, place a stake at the Point of Greatest Pull along each of the directions from which you approach. The place to dig for water would be at the center of these stakes. This practice is better suited for small plots of land. Chapter 6 contains a discussion of how to dowse larger areas.

5 The depth and flow

By now you will have noticed that once the rod has been pulled down and your grip loosened, it will just hang there, lifeless. It is as though a circuit has been broken. At this stage the rod is no longer under the influence of any pull, and it can be easily raised to the starting position for the next operation, which will be determining the depth and the flow of the underground source of water.

Stand at attention over the Point of Greatest Pull just dowsed. With the rod in the starting position and with the tip end slightly higher than level, mark time, lifting your foot about four or five inches from the ground. I have always been intrigued by the fact that it makes no difference how fast or slow one marks time. Pace is unimportant. Only the number of steps is important. Count once for every step—"one, two, three," and so on. While counting you will observe that the tip of the rod will be pulled downward gradually. The number counted when the rod finally reaches a vertical position corresponds to the number of feet that you will have to dig for water. Some dowsers can be off by 10 percent or more between the number of steps taken and the actual depth in feet. Only experience will tell you how to allow for this difference.

Another method of determining depth is to walk backward from the dowsed spot, with the rod held out as before. After a certain number of steps the rod will dip downward. Again, the number of steps taken will determine the depth in feet of the water. Strangely enough, it does not seem to make any difference how small or how large the steps are. It is the number of steps that count.

The amount of water can be determined very often by the strength of the pull. If after counting to thirty the rod dips without much force, place the rod in the starting position and continue counting. The rod will then dip at the next level of water, perhaps at fifty or seventy or one hundred feet, and the strength of the pull will tell you whether or not there is a more abundant supply of water at this level.

With the rod in the starting position, mark time

. . . gradually the tip of the rod is pulled down

. . . one foot of depth for each step taken.

To lay out the field

For the maximum volume of water you should lay out or dowse as large an area as possible. This is done by making a number of passes first in one direction, and then a number of passes in another direction perpendicular to the first series. At each pass, mark the spot where the rod dips down strongly. You will notice that the markers follow a meandering line similar to the path of any brook or stream. And of course this is precisely what happens—except that the markers in this case follow an underground vein or stream. I believe that of all the claims of dowsing, this underground vein theory upsets the geologists the most. If and when you find a location where two or more streams or veins converge or cross, this is the spot to dig for your well.

The drawing at the right shows that the dowser has made five passes from west to east and seven passes from north to south. The pull of the rod will be strongest where the streams cross (designated by the star) and that is the spot to drill.

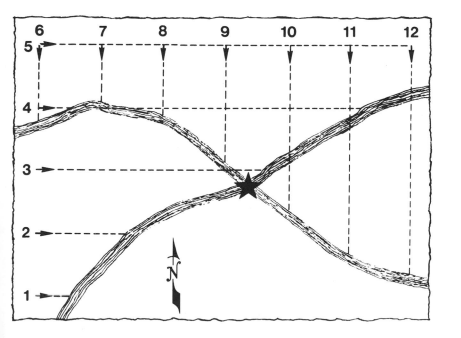

7 **The well digger and you**

Let us suppose that you have dowsed the area and have pinpointed the
spot where the well digger should start. You must first convince him of
the logic of drilling at this particular spot. (Many a well digger chooses
the location of the well by how convenient it is to drive his rig there.)

You must also give him your estimate of the depth so he can slow
down his drilling as he approaches it. If after reaching the proper depth
you find that the volume of water is not sufficient, tell him to dig to the
next level of water.

In dowsing my own farm property I was extremely careful to check
and recheck my findings. When I finally decided on the spot I called the
well digger. I insisted that the point of the drill be placed on the precise
spot I had marked. He raised an eyebrow and politely suppressed a
smile. When I predicted that a good supply of water would be found in
the vicinity of 125 feet down, give or take a few feet, he raised both
eyebrows and could no longer suppress a grin. "Okay, it's your money."
He and his men started drilling. I had to be in the city for a few days, so
I gave him a phone number where I might be reached in case they ran
into any difficulty. Later that week the well digger telephoned. He was
breathless. "All hell broke loose! I think we've hit an underground
river! You have enough water to supply the whole damn town! We
stopped measuring the flow when we hit twenty-five gallons a minute."

The depth of the well was 127 feet. The water was pure, clear, and cold.

There were crystals attached to the drill when it was retracted. The well digger showed these to his brother-in-law, a geology instructor at one of the nearby universities. He identified the crystals as being similar to the stalagmites found on the floors of underground caves. Hardly sufficient evidence for the geologist, but there is an implication here that at least some subsurface water travels in veins.

I think my well digger was converted because he called several months later for help. There was a house in the last stages of construction on a large lot in a town about thirty miles away. The well digger had already sunk three holes to depths of 250 and 300 feet, and all of them had come up dry. I dowsed the property and could not for the life of me get a real tug anywhere. There was a very slight pull at one spot quite close to one of the dry holes. I estimated a very small water supply at about 190 feet. He drilled the spot and came up with three gallons a minute at that depth. Not much of a supply for a large, modern home. The moral of the story: first the water, *then* the house.

After your well is drilled or dug, it is important to have the water tested before drinking. Your state agricultural college, county agent, or a private laboratory can do this for you.

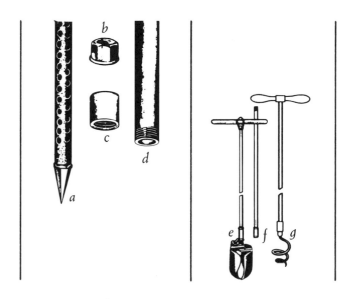

DIGGING YOUR OWN WELL

If you dowse a water source near the surface (less than 25 feet down) you might want to dig, drive, or bore your own well.

Wells that are dug are usually circular in shape, and a pick and shovel are the main tools used. A windlass or hoist and a bucket at the end of a rope are used to bring the earth to the surface. As the hole gets deeper a liner must be inserted to prevent the sides from caving in. The liner can be constructed of stones, bricks, sections of concrete pipe, or even wooden planks properly braced. This liner must extend at least one foot above the ground to prevent surface drain-off, and possibly impure water, from entering the well. A tight cover should be put in place over this liner as additional protection.

Driven wells are constructed by driving a perforated drive point (*a*) into the ground with a sledgehammer. To avoid damage to the threaded end, screw on a driving cap (*b*) which will take the sledge blows. When the drive point has been sunk almost down to its full length, remove the driving cap and attach a coupling (*c*). Thread on to this coupling a length of pipe (*d*). Put the driving cap on top of this extension and continue driving until another extension pipe is needed. Repeat this operation until the drive point reaches the water source.

Bored wells are made with an earth auger (*e*). The auger is turned, forcing the blades into the soil. When the blades are full of earth the auger is pulled up and emptied. Repeat this operation, adding extensions (*f*) as necessary, until the proper depth is reached. If small rocks prevent further boring, the auger is removed from the hole and replaced with a spiral or ram's horn auger (*g*). This type of auger dislodges stones in its path so that they can be brought to the surface. If, however, a large boulder or ledge is encountered, a new location for the well must be found.

If you do decide to drill your own well, let me suggest that you obtain a copy of one of the most helpful books on the subject: *Well Drilling Operations/Army & Air Force Technical Manual.* TM 5–297 AFM 85–23. Though it is currently out of print at the U.S. Government Printing Office, your library may have a copy.

8 Miscellany/Conclusion

Dowsing with the rod as we know it today is at least 400 years old. But it took an event in 1692 in southern France to publicize the art over the length and breadth of Europe. A murder was committed, and the authorities, completely baffled and without a single clue, asked a local dowser to help them find the murderer. The dowser, Jacques Aymar, took rod in hand and proceeded to track down the criminal. The trail was complicated, with many stops and turns, but he soon led the police directly to the hiding place of the culprit. The man confessed to the crime and the details in the confession confirmed in every way the exact route taken by Aymar. Believers and nonbelievers to this day feud over Aymar's achievements, using as weapons articles written hundreds of years after the event. You may or may not believe this man's exploits, but we can all agree that he made dowsing a household word throughout Europe.

This new use of the dowser's rod brought the practice into conflict with the Church. In 1701 the Inquisition, apparently desirous of maintaining its monopoly over unusual methods of determining guilt, decreed that dowsing for missing persons or criminals was definitely out. Of course conflicts between the Church and dowsers were nothing new. Martin Luther had issued a Proclamation branding the use of the rod as a violation of the First Commandment. And in 1658 at Wittenberg it had been officially pronounced that the movements of the dowser's rod were due either to fraud or a strong, binding pact with the devil. More

One of the earliest known illustrations showing the use of the dowsing rod, as it was used to discover precious metals. In the upper right, a man cuts a dowsing rod. In the upper left, a dowser prospects with his rod. To the left, two men point to the find of metal. To the right, a man is digging while below two miners examine the mined metal. From Agricola's *De re metallica*, 1556.

Fred Rodwell using just his hands for dowsing. Woodcut from the English newspaper, *The Graphic*, 1889.

recently, however, the Church and dowsers have had no such conflict. In fact, one of Europe's most celebrated dowsers, the Abbé Mermet, received recognition for his work from the Vatican in May, 1935.

In 1780 a Dr. Thouvenal became interested in the dowsing ability of a young boy by the name of Bleton. The doctor was one of the first men of science to subject the dowser's claims to scientific interpretation. He was ostracized by his colleagues and practically run out of town. To prove how ridiculous this idea of dowsing was, they built a life-size mechanical doll capable of moving an attached rod in the manner of a dowser.

In the late 1800s a fourteen-year-old boy named Rodwell became very well known as a "hand dowser." He would clasp his hands together and proceed to dowse. He knew he was over a vein of water when his hands locked together with great force. He was powerless to separate them until he walked away from the spot. Some observers felt that the boy could actually see the object of this search under the ground. Delrio in his *Folio on Magic*, printed in 1575, tells of meeting a tribe of Spanish Gypsies, the Zahories, who claimed they had the power to see underground water, metals, or buried corpses.

Dowsers can often locate not only water but old wells, septic tanks, underground sewers and pipes, and even basement water tanks (when the dowsing was done on the first floor). As already mentioned, dowsers sometimes have the ability to find lost objects or people. I have heard of dowsers who, after rubbing the tip of their rod with copper, went straightaway to discover a copper mine! Dip the end of your dowsing rod in unrefined oil and you might even discover an oil well.

Other types of dowsing rods and methods suggested for holding them. From an old French work published in 1693.

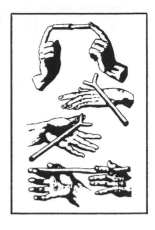

Dowsers have their failures too. An experiment took place in Maine in 1949 that delights the enemies of dowsing. It was performed under the auspices of the American Society for Psychical Research. Twenty-seven dowsers covered a field to select the best spot for sinking a well. They estimated the depth and amount of flow of the water. A geologist and a water engineer went over the same field making their own estimates. Test wells were sunk at all indicated spots. The geologist and the engineer did fairly well at estimating the depth, but not the volume. The diviners did poorly at both depth and volume. But the poor showing that dowsers sometimes make in "controlled" experiments should not discourage the dowser. We know too little about the forces inherent in the art to set the proper controls. I'm reminded of the early days of photography, when skeptics claimed that it was all an enormous hoax. If it wasn't a fraud, they argued, why did so much of the activity have to be conducted in a dark room.

The Abbé Mermet, one of Europe's great dowsers, writes of one of his failures in his classic *Principles and Practice of Radiesthesia*. On March 4, 1933, he was in Switzerland on a dowsing commission when he became aware that his rod did not move during the entire time. He finally left, remarking that "there is something very serious happening in the atmosphere today." The next morning the papers carried the news of one of the most destructive tidal waves that ever hit Japan. Is there a correlation? Was there some unnoticed physical or atmospheric disturbance occurring at the time of the Maine experiment? We don't know. Why dowsers fail is still just as much a mystery as why they succeed.

MAP DOWSING

Some dowsers insist that dowsing has nothing to do with static electricity or any other phenomenon of physics. They believe it is a psychic experience closely related to some kind of mental radar. They believe that this enables them to dowse over maps and discover water or minerals sometimes thousands of miles away. Part of this technique consists of asking the dowsing rod pertinent questions. With the rod held in the starting position you say to yourself (or out loud if no one is nearby!), "Is the water over ten feet down?" If the rod does not move ask, "Is it over fifteen feet down?" If the rod starts to dip, ask, "Is it over twenty feet down?" If the rod does not move you are sure that the water is between fifteen and twenty feet down. You then count from fifteen to twenty, asking at each number if this is the right depth. The rod should dip at that number which corresponds to the depth of the water.

This technique may be used to ask all sorts of questions of the rod, such as "Is the water pure?" or "Is a ledge present to make digging or boring difficult?" If the rod remains in the starting position, the answer is, of course, no. If the rod dips the answer is yes. This method of divining can be used out in the field as well as indoors over maps.

Even I find map dowsing difficult to believe. But then I think back to my own skepticism of the whole subject of dowsing and I wonder.

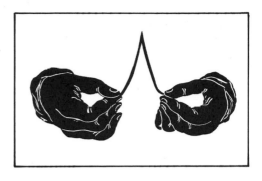

Pocket-size dowsing rod of aluminum used in the late nineteenth century in England.

GAMES DOWSERS PLAY

If two or more dowsers are present, the following routine can be both fun and impressive to nonbelievers. One dowser, completely hidden from the view of the other, walks in a straight line until the rod dips. Mark this spot carefully in such a manner so that the other dowser will not be able to see the marker. Continue in this way until the first dowser has marked off four or five spots. If you now start the second dowser on the same path, his rod will invariably dip at the same spots that were selected by the first dowser. This is a pretty strong argument against those who still believe that it's all a fraud.

Here is an indoor variation. Commandeer a half-dozen buckets or any type of waterproof containers. Fill just one with water. Put them in a row and cover each one so as to make it impossible to detect the empty ones from the one containing water. Now try to dowse the bucket with the water.

The art connoisseur, Bernard Berenson, in his *Rumor and Reflection*, writes of a game played by a well-known Italian dowser who completely astonished him one evening. A number of photographs of paintings by the Old Masters were spread out on a table, face down. The dowser, with the guidance of a wand or pendulum, proceeded to make neat little piles of all the photographs, face down. The piles were then turned face up and each pile consisted of all the paintings done by the same artist. Berenson remarked that he had studied art for years before he could do that, and then only if all the pictures were face up!

Some years ago an oil geologist devised a test for those who called themselves oil dowsers, but it has all the makings of a good game. Ten cigar boxes were filled with sand, and one box contained a small bottle of oil buried in the sand. The boxes were then shuffled and spread out on the floor, ready for the dowser to select the box containing the oil. After each dowsing the boxes were reshuffled, and this was done ten times. The geologist felt that if a dowser could find oil thousands of feet down he most certainly could spot it three feet away. If any dowser correctly dowsed all ten times he would receive financial backing to sink his own well. Some fifty dowsers tried it and I'm sorry to report that the highest score was three correct dowsings out of ten. Try it, either as a game or a serious test of your abilities. Instead of oil try minerals, precious metals, or gems.

Dowsers are sometimes capable of transmitting their power to another person. Have a nondowser hold the rod in the starting position. Now if a dowser holds on to the wrists of the nondowser, quite often the rod will dip over a likely spot. The nondowser seems to tune in on the wavelength of the dowser.

It is always interesting when two dowsers meet, particularly when one

Another technique is to use a wire coat hanger, bending two pieces into L shapes. Put the shorter legs of the wires into two pipes so they can revolve easily. Start in the position shown with the wires out straight. As you approach a vein of water the wires will swing to the sides a full ninety degrees.

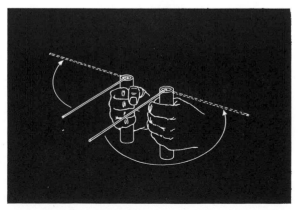

of them dowses with the rod going up. Walking together side by side, each dowser holds one end of the forked twig. When they come upon a likely spot, half the rod tries to go up while the other half tries to go down, and the result is a wild wobbling.

Dowsing can contribute enormously to your outdoor fun, and it isn't always necessary to prove by digging that every dowsed spot has water below. The phenomenon of the rod consistently being forced down at certain spots—and only those spots—is in itself a mysterious, fascinating experience for anyone to witness.

For those who are interested, there is an organization of dowsers open to anyone, dowsers and nondowsers alike. The American Society of Dowsers, Inc., is a nonprofit educational and scientific society. Members receive the organization's quarterly, *The American Dowser*, which always contains interesting articles on the subject. Write to American Society of Dowsers, Inc., Danville, Vermont 05828.

I hope that after reading this book and following the directions you will experience the thrill of discovering that you are a dowser. And whether you go into the business of locating veins of water or minerals, or use dowsing just as an outdoor hobby, you have learned something important—that we are still surrounded by mysteries here on earth which, at present, cannot be explained.

The author has been dowsing as a hobby for over twenty-five years in Connecticut and western Massachusetts with phenomenal success. He has yet to see a dry hole wherever the well digger has followed his directions. He has dowsed for farmers and vacation homeowners. They are still drinking pure, sparkling water and they are still very grateful to him for discovering it.

One farmer, even to this day, never misses an opportunity to express his gratitude. And for good reason. It seems that the well digger suggested a spot for drilling that was almost 150 feet from the house with an estimated depth of 150 to 200 feet. The author dowsed the area and found that the spot to drill was 10 feet from the house and about 35 feet down. The well was drilled, the water came in at 35 feet, and the farmer and his family are still enjoying the water. The well has never run dry, and that was over twenty years ago.

The author has never charged a cent for his dowsing services. When grateful homeowners ask him for his bill, his usual answer is, "No charge. Folks should never have to pay for pure drinking water!"